COPYRIGHT PAGE

This Too... A Companion Journal by Natalie Friscia Pancetti

Published by IG Introspections, an imprint of Inspired Girl Publishing Group, a division of Inspired Girl Enterprises.
Asbury Park, NJ
www.inspiredgirlbooks.com

Inspired Girl Books is honored to bring forth books with heart and stories that matter. We are proud to offer this book to our readers; the theme, the life- isms, the thoughts, and the words are the author's alone. The author and publisher do not assume and hereby disclaim any liability in connection with the use of the information contained in this book.

For permissions contact:
help@inspiredgirlbooks.com.

ISBN: 978-1-965240-05-2
Editorial and Creative Direction by Jenn Tuma-Young
Written by Natalie Friscia Pancetti
Author Photo by Jessica Morrisy Photography

Printed in the USA.

THIS *too*...

A COMPANION JOURNAL

By Natalie Friscia Pancetti

THIS *too...*

REALIZING

the Days

MAY FEEL LONG
AND
TIRESOME,

but the years are short
and pass quickly.

Bucket List

Write a list of 7 things you'd like to experience in your lifetime.

1.

_____

_____

_____

2.

_____

_____

_____

3.

_____

_____

_____

4.

5.

6.

7.

Count your blessings...

How can a comfort zone be a danger zone?

THIS *too*...

PRAY, LISTEN, AND

Breathe

BECAUSE
THOSE ARE THE
BASIC NEEDS

to sustain and appreciate

another day.

Gratitude List

Write a list of **7** things you are most
grateful for in this moment.

1.

2.

3.

4.

5.

6.

7.

How do you define success?

_____

_____

_____

_____

_____

_____

_____

_____

_____

_____

_____

_____

_____

_____

_____

_____

_____

_____

_____

_____

_____

_____

_____

_____

_____

_____

_____

_____

_____

_____

_____

_____

_____

_____

_____

_____

_____

_____

_____

_____

_____

What do you love about yourself?

THIS *too*...

LENDING A

Helping

Hand

WITH A FULL
HEART

is actually also helping
ourselves.

Donation List

Write a list of 7 ways you can contribute, volunteer, and give back in your community.

1.

_____
_____
_____

2.

_____
_____
_____

3.

_____
_____
_____

4.

5.

6.

7.

What wisdom can you share today?

_____

_____

_____

_____

_____

_____

_____

_____

_____

_____

_____

_____

_____

_____

_____

_____

_____

_____

_____

_____

Give yourself grace for being human.

THIS *too...*

INSTEAD OF BEING
YOUR OWN

Worst

Enemy

HOW ABOUT BEING
YOUR OWN BEST
FRIEND

and talking to yourself as you
would to that dear friend?

Self-Love List

Write a list of 7 things you
love about yourself.

1.
_____
_____
_____

2.
_____
_____
_____

3.
_____
_____
_____

4. _____

5. _____

6. _____

7. _____

What struggle led you to your greatest success?

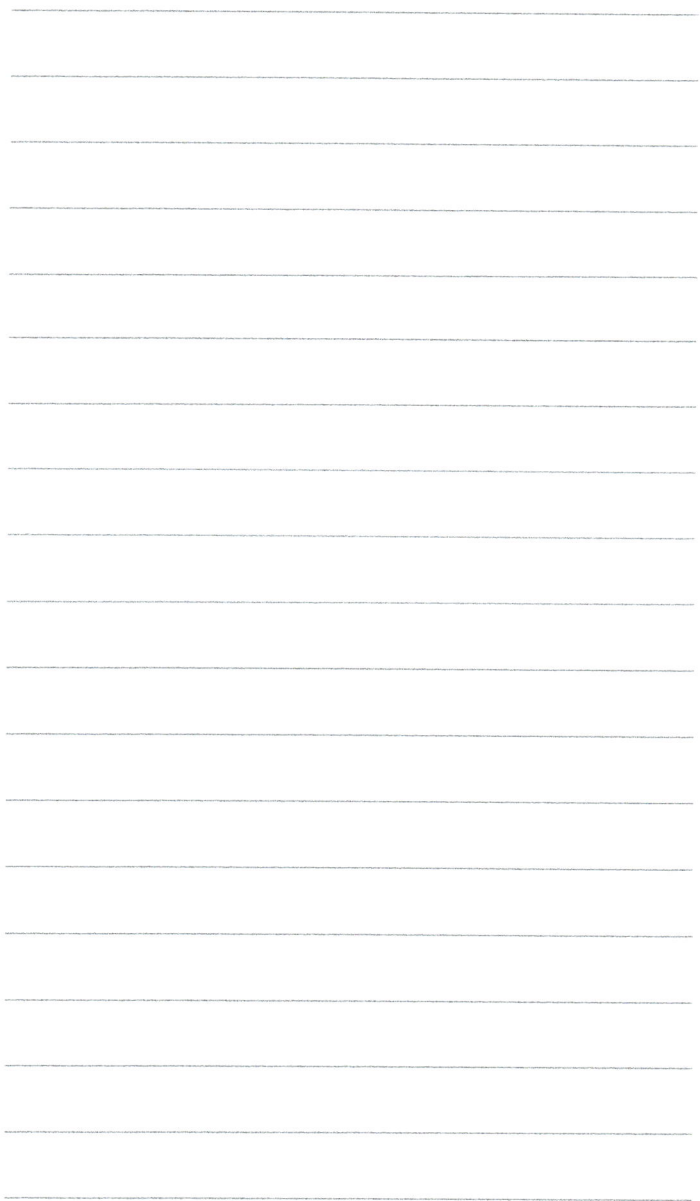

Overthinking makes bad situations worse.

THIS *too...*

WAKE UP WITH A

Purpose

A REAL INTENTION THAT BRINGS YOUR SOUL JOY.

Accomplishing this makes everything else seem so much better.

Goal List

Write a list of **7** current goals you
are working toward.

1. _____
   _____
   _____

2. _____
   _____
   _____

3. _____
   _____
   _____

4.

_____

_____

_____

5.

_____

_____

_____

6.

_____

_____

_____

7.

_____

_____

_____

Shine a lost loved ones light through you.

Look around at all you have done.
What are you proud of?

THIS *too...*

ALLOW WHAT
WILL BE,

Strive

FOR WHAT YOU
WANT,

and hope for the best.

Wish List

Write a list of **7** things you desire
or are praying about.

1. _____
   _____
   _____

2. _____
   _____
   _____

3. _____
   _____
   _____

4. _____

_____

_____

5. _____

_____

_____

6. _____

_____

_____

7. _____

_____

_____

What is your passion?

_____

_____

_____

_____

_____

_____

_____

_____

_____

_____

_____

_____

_____

_____

_____

_____

_____

_____

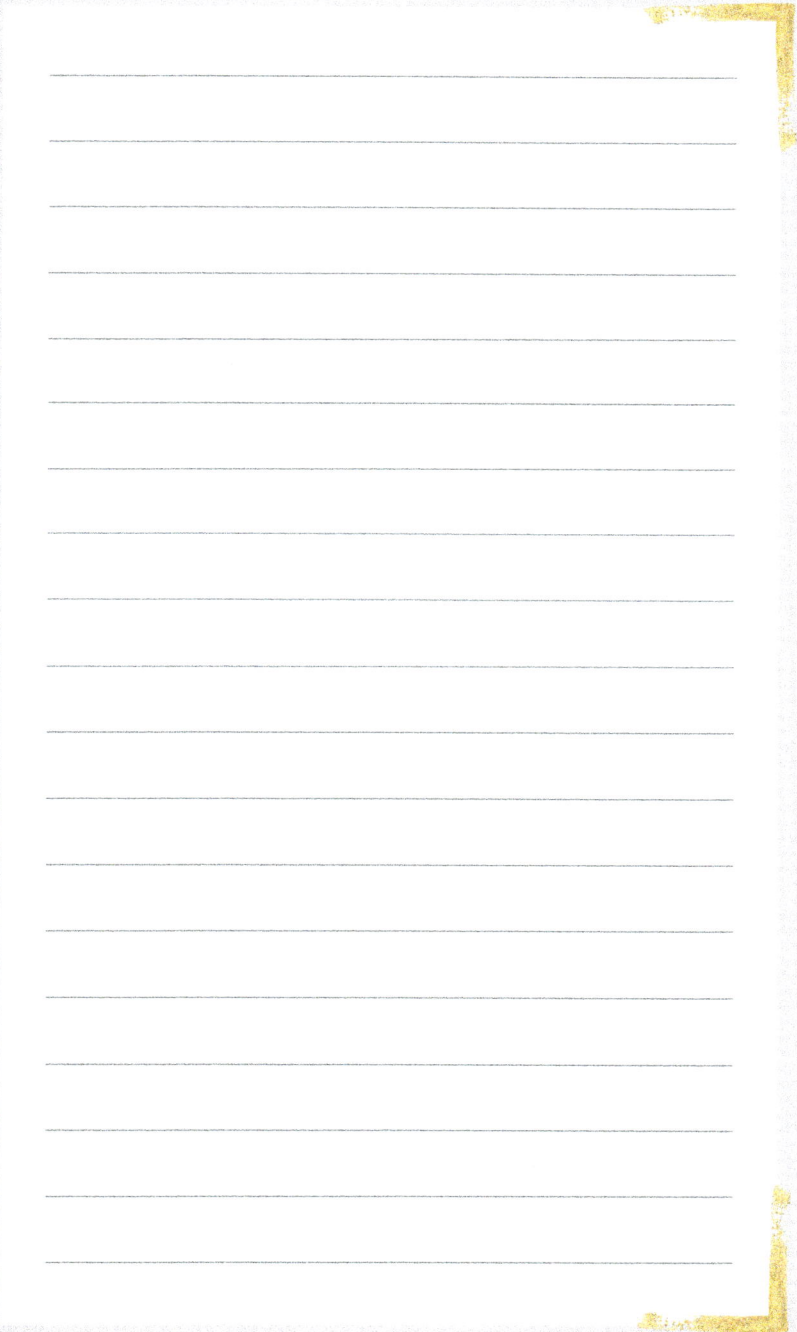

_____

_____

_____

_____

_____

_____

_____

_____

_____

_____

_____

_____

_____

_____

_____

_____

_____

_____

_____

_____

_____

_____

How do you deal with disappointment?

THIS *too...*

REMEMBER THAT
THE "LAST" OF
SOMETHING ALWAYS
BRINGS THE

Hopeful
Opportunity

TO ENJOY
THE FIRST OF
SOMETHING ELSE.

Embrace the blessing of that
change in your life.

Butterfly List

Write a list of **7** ways you are transforming,
changing, and growing.

1.
_____
_____
_____

2.
_____
_____
_____

3.
_____
_____
_____

4.

5.

6.

7.

What will your legacy be?

_____

_____

_____

_____

_____

_____

_____

_____

_____

_____

_____

_____

_____

_____

_____

_____

_____

How have you been tested?

www.ingramcontent.com/pod-product-compliance
Lightning Source LLC
Chambersburg PA
CBHW050020090426
42734CB00021B/3345